Skinnygirl
COCKTAILS

100
fun & flirty
guilt-free recipes

BETHENNY FRANKEL

A TOUCHSTONE BOOK
Published by Simon & Schuster
New York   London   Toronto   Sydney   New Delhi

Touchstone
A Division of Simon & Schuster, Inc.
1230 Avenue of the Americas
New York, NY 10020

Copyright © 2014 by Big Talk, LLC

Photography copyright © 2014 by Lucy Schaeffer

Material in this book was previously published in *The Skinnygirl Dish*
and *Skinnygirl Solutions*.

Skinnygirl Cocktails is a registered trademark of Jim Beam Brands Co.
and is used under authorized license to Big Talk, LLC.
All rights reserved worldwide.

First Touchstone trade paperback edition October 2014

TOUCHSTONE and colophon are registered trademarks of
Simon & Schuster, Inc.

For information about special discounts for bulk purchases,
please contact Simon & Schuster Special Sales at 1-866-506-1949 or
business@simonandschuster.com.

The Simon & Schuster Speakers Bureau can bring authors to your
live event. For more information or to book an event, contact the
Simon & Schuster Speakers Bureau at 1-866-248-3049 or visit our
website at www.simonspeakers.com.

Interior design by Akasha Archer
Cover design by Laurie Carkett
Cover photograph © Lucy Schaeffer

Manufactured in the United States of America

10   9   8   7   6   5   4   3   2   1

Library of Congress Cataloging-in-Publication Data

Frankel, Bethenny.
   Skinnygirl cocktails : 100 fun and flirty guilt-free recipes/ Bethenny
Frankel.
      pages   cm
   "A Touchstone Book."
   Includes index.
   1. Cocktails.   2. Low-calorie diet—Recipes.   I. Title.
   TX951.F73   2014
   641.87′4—dc23   2014012642

ISBN 978-1-4767-7302-5
ISBN 978-1-4767-7303-2 (ebook)

CONTENTS

DRINK LIKE A SKINNYGIRL

I f you know me, you know that whether I'm at a fancy Hollywood party, at a happy hour with friends, or just relaxing after a long day, I love a cocktail. But what I don't love is that the usual drinks are packed with needless calories. Take frozen margaritas—they usually have between 500 and 1,000 calories! That's why I first invented my now-famous Skinnygirl Margarita, which only has 100 calories per serving. It's also why I've created all the recipes in this book. I make cocktails that will satisfy you with their flavor, but they're cocktails you can trust. They all have far fewer calories than most regular drinks—many of them are under 150 calories—but they still taste so delicious that you'll want another one . . . and maybe even another one after that!

Here's the thing: drinking like a Skinnygirl does not mean depriving yourself of the cocktails you love—it just means being smart about what you put in them. Using a lot of sugary mixers can make drinks fattening, but as I've shown with my hugely successful line of Ready-to-Drink cocktails, they don't have to be that way! I love taking a drink that would normally be loaded down with sugar and calories and making it so you can enjoy it guilt-free. The recipes in this book will show you how to get the full flavor that you crave without all the extra calories. *You can have your cocktail and drink it, too.*

The secret to drinking my way is the Skinnygirl Fixologist Formula. It's a quick and easy way to make any drink with just a fraction of the calories. Once you know it, you can go wild and create a Skinnygirl version of any cocktail you want. So memorize it, and use it.

Skinnygirl Fixologist Formula

1. Fill a rocks glass with ice. As the ice melts, the extra water will help keep you hydrated, and you'll be able to sip the drink for longer—every little bit counts!

2. Add a shot of clear liquor. Measure with a shot glass or just pour while counting one . . . two. I always try to drink clear liquor because it's cleaner and lighter than dark liquor. I swear by vodka and white tequila, since it's so easy to make a vodka or tequila version of almost any drink. Gin also works, and so does light rum. All liquors that don't have added sugar have the same amount of calories.

3. Fill the rocks glass almost the rest of the way up with club soda or seltzer. This is a good zero-calorie filler that doesn't bring an overly strong flavor. Plus, it reduces the strength of the drink and helps keep you hydrated. Be careful, though, you don't want to shake soda. So if you're making a cocktail that gets mixed in a cocktail shaker, add the bubbles after you've shaken the rest of the drink and strained it into the glass.

4. Add just a splash of the sweet or fruity component that gives the drink its character. Typically this will be a sweet liqueur, sugary mixer, or fruit juice, but whatever it is go very light. You just want to give enough flavor to accent the drink. Instead of ordering a regular vodka cranberry, order a vodka and soda with just a splash of cranberry and add a lime to make it interesting. I always like to add fresh fruit as a garnish whenever possible.

And that's it. It's so simple. You'll thank yourself when you wake up clear-eyed in the morning and can still button your jeans!

Of course, it's not just about what you're drinking. It's about how you drink it, too. As I always say, you can have it all, just not all at once—and that's how I approach going out. If you follow a few simple rules, you'll avoid the overindulgences that can lead to late-night regrets and nasty hangovers.

- Let's be clear. Dark liquor has more impurities than clear, and that's a one-way ticket to hangover city. So stick to the clear stuff—and be careful not to end up with flavored vodkas and rums that are secretly sugary. Obviously, I recommend using products from my Skinnygirl line since we don't add extra sugar. My drinks are always naturally sweetened and low-calorie, but of course you can use any liquor brand you trust.

- Know how much you can drink and give yourself a maximum number of drinks. I generally try to have no more than two drinks a night. I obviously bend this rule from time to time, but for me it's a good goal to shoot for.

- Stay hydrated. Drink a glass of water or club soda for every alcoholic drink you consume. Make alternating between water and booze your unbreakable personal policy! I don't manage to do this every time, but I always try. It also helps to order things on a lot of rocks because as the ice melts you can drink it, too.

- Watch out for those sneaky wine refills. Wine is delicious (especially my Skinnygirl wine collection), but it can go down more quickly than a mixed drink. Be extra careful when you're at a dinner party or wedding and someone is constantly topping off your wineglass—it's a recipe for drinking too much without realizing it. A cocktail will give you more control, because you can sip and you won't get more unless you order another one. But if you do want wine, simply ask your host or server not to refill your glass until it's empty. That way you can keep track of how many glasses you've had.

- Beware of super sweet mixers. Frozen cocktails are a trap! They're nothing but colored sugar. Stay away from them if you can. But if you're at a party and you end up with an entire glass full of piña colada from a machine, treat it like you would a decadent dessert: take a few sips and then put it down. Or better yet, ask the bartender to follow the Fixologist Formula. So you'd modify a margarita by asking for a tequila and soda and then asking the bartender to top off the drink with just a splash of the frozen margarita mix.

- The same goes for super sweet dessert liqueurs. If you want to enjoy a glass of one after dinner, by all means do—but reduce its caloric punch by mixing it with vodka and soda over ice. Make it more of a splash on top than the whole drink, and use it in place of one of your cocktail hour drinks or as a replacement for dessert. Or you could pour it over a lot of ice, sip it slowly, and not finish it all. There's no hard-and-fast rule; you just want to be sure you're not overdoing it on the sugar.

- Avoid late-night snacking. Drinking is fun, but what's not so fun is when you get home and end up eating everything in sight. Your judgment is one of the first things to go when you drink, and that makes it tough to stick to your plan when you get home. The key is to eat well all day long so you're not starving—and be careful not to skip dinner! But if you do still feel like a snack, remember to check yourself before you wreck yourself. Make a smart, balanced choice. Edamame is better than pizza or cookies. Though if you've avoided sweets all day and kept a lid on your alcohol consumption, it's fine to have a bit of dessert.

Nobody's perfect! Don't beat yourself up if you don't follow every rule every time, but use these as your partying guidelines, and you'll be having tons of fun without waking up sorry the next day.

LET'S PARTY!

Okay, you've got the basics down. Now you're ready to get your drink on! I have gathered my best cocktail recipes and party tips in this book. It is packed with drinks that will help you throw the ultimate Skinnygirl party. Whether you're just having your BFF over for some one-on-one time or you're having the whole neighborhood over, I've got you covered.

Some advice: as a former event planner, I know the most important thing you can do when throwing a party of any size is to have a theme. Some might be obvious to your guests, like Halloween or the Super Bowl, but the theme doesn't have to be in your face—it can just be something you keep in your head so you know what you're after when you're selecting the food, drinks, decor, music, and lighting.

The other key to a successful party is having a signature cocktail. Premix it in pitchers and let your guests help themselves. Most people will be more than happy to drink whatever you're serving, and having just one option—or two, if it's a really big party—eliminates the expense and hassle of stocking a full bar. Plus, it saves you from the sticky mess of people mixing their own drinks, which always ends in a table crowded with half-empty bottles and bottle caps.

Pick a signature cocktail that goes with the party's theme and that will appeal to the majority of your guests. Just remember that red drinks stain—so if that's a problem with your furniture or rugs, don't pick a red wine or cranberry cocktail! (Though you can always substitute in white cranberry juice.) I like to get an inexpensive picture frame and fill it with a printed-out description of the evening's cocktail. Or you can write the menu on a chalkboard that you set behind the bar. Just do something so that people know what they're drinking.

All of the recipes in this book can easily be scaled up to make larger amounts. (Except where noted, each recipe makes a single serving; just multiply the quantities by the number of drinks you want to serve.) Mix the cocktail ahead of time in a pitcher, but don't put in any ice, since it will melt and dilute the drink. Then when your guests arrive, set out the pitchers with glasses, garnishes, and buckets of ice, and let people serve themselves. Chilling glasses ahead of time, especially beer mugs and martini glasses, is a nice touch. And don't forget to put out pitchers of water (with some lemons and/or limes) and water glasses so your guests can stay hydrated!

BUILDING YOUR OWN BAR

Whether you're serving a signature cocktail to a crowd or just mixing up a margarita for yourself, having a well-stocked bar makes drinking well at home so much easier. It also saves time and money when you're entertaining: you'll already have what you need to mix your signature cocktail, people can pour their own drinks, and you won't have to pay a bartender.

I personally love storing everything together on an elegant bar cart. It's a chic way to display your liquor, glasses, and accessories, and it's neater and cleaner to have everything in one spot. Here's a list of things that are useful to have, but don't feel like you need to get them all at once. Collect them over time, and you'll end up with a home bar that makes whipping up your favorite Skinnygirl cocktail a breeze.

Tools

- **Glasses.** Rocks glasses are my go-to glass. They're not too big, and they work for almost any drink. All-purpose glasses with a stem also work well for both wine and cocktails. It's nice to have a few other options around, like tall (highball) glasses and martini glasses, for serving special drinks, but it's not strictly necessary.

- **A pitcher,** for serving drinks to a group.

- **An ice bucket,** for when people are pouring their own drinks.

- **A small cutting board or bar board,** for cutting fruit.

- **A sharp knife,** for cutting lemon and lime wedges and peels.

- **A cocktail shaker.** This isn't a must-have, but a shaker comes with most bar tool sets. They are great for making delightfully cold cocktails.

- **A muddler.** I like the natural wooden ones, but they come in different materials like metal, too. You can use them to muddle berries, mint, citrus, or whatever you want, to add flavor to your drink. (See "Muddle This," page 15.) It's not absolutely necessary, but it's fun.

- **A long-handled mixing spoon.** These are usually long silver spoons, and they often come in bar tool sets. But use any spoon that's long enough to let you stir drinks in a shaker or pitcher.

- **A cocktail rimmer.** This makes rimming a glass with salt or sugar super easy. You can also do it in a small plate (see "Rim Shot," page 7), but a rimmer allows you to store the salt/sugar in between uses.

- **Reusable ice cubes or whiskey stones.** These are nice to have when you don't want melting ice diluting your drink.

- **A corkscrew.** Choose any kind you like and know how to use.

- **Cute cocktail napkins.** These are really convenient to have, and they also add a nice touch of color to any bar cart.

- Coasters. Choose some that go well with your decor, and don't be shy about using them—they'll stop your guests from making sticky rings on all your furniture.

- A champagne bucket. This is an easy and elegant way to keep your bubbly or white wine chilled while you're serving it.

> ┌─ RIM SHOT ─────────────────────────────
>
> Rimming a glass with salt, sugar, crushed candy, or spicy chili powder is a cute way to add more flavor. It makes any drink more fun, and it's super simple to do: Put out one small plate with a bit of water or lime juice on it. Lay out another plate with whatever you're using on the rim of the glass. Dip the top of your glass in the water or juice first, then dip it in the sugar (or whatever coating you're using) until the rim is well coated. Pour in the drink, and you've got yourself a classy-looking cocktail.

Liquor and Embellishments

You definitely don't need to have every liquor option ever on your bar cart. Start with a few basics and then add special liqueurs and mixers as you discover them.

- One or two bottles of your favorite clear liquor. I, of course, recommend a few bottles of my Skinnygirl Vodka (which comes naked and in a variety of flavors), but you could choose any kind of vodka, 100% agave clear tequila, light (clear) rum, or gin.

- One bottle of citrus liqueur, such as Cointreau, triple sec, or Grand Marnier, for margaritas.

- One or two bottles of different fun liqueurs, for flavoring your favorite cocktails (such as peach schnapps, apple, Midori, etc.).

- Juices, for making your favorite drinks. Have one or two, like orange, cranberry, or grapefruit, around all the time, and buy others if you need them for a special cocktail.

- Garnishes. The classics, of course, are lemons, limes, oranges, a jar of cherries, and a jar of martini olives. For a special theme or occasion, you might want to add a little extra sweetness to your drinks. Candied orange peel (see "Gorgeous Garnishes," page 77) or even real candy add a nice touch—think gummy worms, peppermints, candy corn, or anything that matches your drink of choice.

- Sugar, for garnishing glass rims. Or raw sugar, if you want a healthier, less-processed option. Places like Williams-Sonoma sell flavored colored sugars that are made for this purpose and can be fun.

- Honey, agave nectar, or homemade Simple Syrup, for sweetening drinks (see below).

- A few bottles of club soda and/or seltzer. Also keep tonic water or diet soda around if you like them.

- Plenty of ice.

THE SIMPLEST SYRUP

Simple syrup gives a delicious hint of sweetness and is used in a lot of cocktails. It is also used as the base for sour mix (see page 17), so it's good to have plenty on hand.

Simple Syrup

1 part sugar (not artificial sweetener)
3 parts hot water

Put the sugar in a cup or bowl and pour the hot water over it. Stir until all the sugar has dissolved. Store it in a sealed container in the fridge so you have it handy.

Now you have everything you need to throw an amazing party. Just let me give you one final piece of advice: don't stress. The recipes are all low-calorie and delicious as they are, but don't worry about following them exactly. The calorie counts are based on each recipe as it's written, but it's no problem if you want to use a different brand of liquor or mixer. For instance, I often suggest that you use one of my Skinnygirl Vodkas or other drinks from my line in a recipe. The vodkas come in different flavors—Bare Naked, Cucumber, Meyer Lemon, Tangerine, and White Cherry—but you don't have to use the exact liquor I've put in the recipe. Pick whatever brand you trust and experiment with different flavors. Same goes for my Skinnygirl Sparklers, which are available in Pink Grapefruit, Pineapple Coconut, Tangerine Mango, and Strawberry Lemonade. They have just 5 calories per serving, so I like to use them as mixers. But if you don't have them on hand, just use your favorite club soda, sparkling water, or even diet soda.

You also don't need to go crazy measuring each ounce out to the drop. In fact, I usually just like to count one . . . two while pouring a shot rather than measuring at all. I'm all about mixing and matching and finding clever substitutions along the way. I've created these drinks to inspire you, but please play with them as you go and make them your own.

Cheers!

MARVELOUS
MARGARITAS

“

I created the Skinnygirl Margarita because I wanted to have a signature cocktail that I could drink when I was out that wouldn't leave me feeling bloated and hungover the next day. I didn't want to just drink plain tequila or vodka. So I decided to make a version of the margarita that was fun and enjoyable but that I could trust to be low in calories with just a hint of sweetness. Pretty soon the nation was on fire for my margarita, and bartenders were telling me it was their most popular cocktail. It's delicious, of course, but I also love it because you can change up the flavors so easily and have fun creating your own signature cocktails.

classic margarita

*under 150 calories

After I made this drink famous on *The Real Housewives of New York City*, it became so popular that I launched my Skinnygirl Ready-to-Drink Cocktail line with it. Here's the at-home version that couldn't be easier to make.

2 ounces white (clear) tequila (100% agave)

Small splash of triple sec or other orange or citrus liqueur

Large splash of fresh lime juice or 4 lime wedges

Splash of club soda, to lighten it (optional)

Lime wheel, for garnish

Combine the tequila, triple sec, and lime juice in a rocks glass filled with ice. (If you're using lime wedges, squeeze them into the glass.) Top it off with club soda, if you like, and stir to combine. Garnish with a lime wheel.

VARIATIONS: You can also make this into virtually any fruit flavor you want by adding a splash of juice. Try grapefruit, orange, pomegranate, or anything else that sounds tasty.

JUICE IT UP

It's traditional to rim your glass by using a bit of lime juice on a small plate. But if you want to add extra flair to your cocktail service, change it up and get your juice straight from the fruit you're using in the drink. For a grapefruit margarita, simply cut a grapefruit in half, then slice the bottom off one side and place that on a plate. Then press the top of the glass into the fruit's flesh until the rim is coated with juice. Then dip it in salt or sugar or whatever you like. This trick also works well with oranges, lemons, and limes.

spicy jalapeño margarita
*under 150 calories

Hot and peppery, this drink is perfect for celebrating Cinco de Mayo—or for any time you want to bring a little caliente kick to your party.

Two ¼-inch slices jalapeño chile, seeds removed (use more slices if you like it spicy)

3 ounces Skinnygirl Ready-to-Drink Margarita*

Chili powder or Mexican chili seasoning mixed with coarse salt, for rimming the glass

Lime peel, for garnish

Muddle the jalapeño slices in the bottom of a cocktail shaker. Pour the Skinnygirl Margarita cocktail over the jalapeños. Add ice and shake well. Rim a rocks glass with the chili powder mixture and pour in the margarita. Garnish with a lime peel.

* Some people like a stronger drink, so add a splash of tequila if you want.

MUDDLE THIS

Muddling is a bartending technique that involves bruising citrus peels, berries, peppers, or herbs like mint or cilantro leaves so that they release their natural essential oils and give flavor to a drink. You can buy a muddler (which looks like a tapered stick with a blunt end) or you can use a metal or wooden spoon or a pestle if you have a mortar and pestle. To do it, put the ingredients to be muddled in the bottom of a thick glass or cocktail shaker and smash them around with the muddler. Add the rest of the drink's ingredients and stir or shake. It's that easy!

frozen mango margarita

Frozen margarita mixes are usually made with crazy amounts of sugar, but my version is a fresh, cool treat that won't load you down with calories. You can make this into any flavor you want by simply using a different fruit puree.

1¼ ounces white (clear) tequila (100% agave)

½ ounce triple sec or other orange or citrus liqueur

2 ounces lemon-lime Sour Mix (below)

1 ounce mango puree (or ¼ cup frozen mango)

Lime wheel, for garnish

Fill the glass you're serving the drink in with ice, then dump the ice into a blender. Add the tequila, triple sec, sour mix, and blend until smooth. Pour into the glass. Garnish with a lime wheel on the rim.

SWEET AND SOUR

Sour mix is a great way to add a little citrus-y punch to a drink—I use it in a lot of these recipes. By varying the juice, you can make lemon sour, lime sour, or combine the two for lemon-lime sour.

Sour Mix
2 parts fresh lemon or lime juice
1 part Simple Syrup (page 8)

Pour the juice and simple syrup into a jar or bowl. Stir to combine. Store any leftovers in a sealed container in the fridge.

pucker up margarita

This flashy margarita has an awesome sweet-and-sour punch.

1½ ounces white (clear) tequila (100% agave)

½ ounce melon liqueur or any flavor of Pucker liqueur

2 ounces lemon-lime Sour Mix (page 17)

Piece of orange slice candy or other sour fruit candy, for garnish

Combine the tequila, liqueur, and sour mix in a rocks glass filled with ice. Garnish with an orange slice candy on the rim—or you could even float a Sour Patch Kid or two in the drink!

VARIATION: To make this a frozen margarita, first fill the glass you're serving it in with ice. Dump the ice into the blender, add the rest of the ingredients, and blend until smooth. Pour into the glass and garnish.

TRUST YOUR TASTE BUDS

If you order a muffin and discover that it tastes exactly like cake, you instantly know it's loaded with sugar and you stop eating it. It's the same thing with sugary drinks—you know when you taste something if you can trust it. So if you get a syrupy sweet margarita at a Mexican restaurant, send it back and ask for a tequila on the rocks with just a splash of margarita mix on top instead. Remember, you can always use the Skinnygirl Fixologist Formula to end up with the right mix of sweet and sparkle.

FUN & FLIRTY
MARTINIS

" "

You can never go wrong with a martini. It's the quintessential cocktail, and every Skinnygirl should know how to make one. Traditional vodka and gin martinis are naturally low in calories. (Just beware of getting too down and dirty with the olive juice, since it's loaded with sodium and causes bloating.) Other versions of the martini can be surprisingly high in sugar, but they don't have to be. These sexy twists on the classic are guaranteed to get things shaking without stirring up any guilt the next morning.

old hollywood

*under 150 calories

A Skinnygirl take on a timeless cocktail.

2 ounces Skinnygirl Bare Naked Vodka or other unflavored vodka

Splash of dry vermouth

Martini olives, for garnish

Combine the vodka and vermouth with ice in a cocktail shaker and shake well. Strain into a chilled martini glass. Garnish with olives on a pick.

THE ICE QUEEN

Have you ever wondered how steakhouses and martini bars get those little bits of ice floating on the top of their drinks? It took me years to figure this out! I finally discovered that if you rinse your glasses and put them in the freezer, when the drink hits the ice in the glass, you get the bits of floating ice on top. Try it at home—it's like magic!

lychee martini

*under 150 calories

When I was on *The Real Housewives of New York City*, I made these for my girlfriends, and they were a big hit.

1½ ounces vodka

1 ounce lychee juice*

1 ounce club soda

2 or 3 lychees, for garnish

Combine the vodka and lychee juice with ice in a cocktail shaker and shake well. Strain into a chilled martini glass. Top off with the club soda. Garnish with lychees.

*You can buy canned lychees at a supermarket or Asian grocery.

VARIATION: If you want to make these look really fancy, rub the rim of the glass with fresh ginger and dip it in colored sugar.

gin & juice
*under 150 calories

Cool and refreshing, this gin martini is wonderful on its own, but it also pairs perfectly with oysters or a shrimp cocktail.

1¼ ounces gin, or vodka if you prefer it

1 ounce fresh lemon juice

1 ounce cucumber juice*

½ ounce Simple Syrup (page 8)

Cucumber slice, for garnish

Combine the gin, lemon juice, cucumber juice, and simple syrup with ice in a cocktail shaker and shake well. Strain into a chilled martini glass. Garnish with a cucumber slice on the rim.

*You can make this by putting a peeled cucumber through a juicer. Or you can muddle 4 to 6 pieces peeled cucumber (1/2-inch slices) and double-strain the juice (using both the cocktail strainer and a small sieve) before using.

sake-tini
*under 150 calories

Sake, a Japanese drink made from fermented rice, makes a martini that tastes both exquisite and exotic. Like wine, sake comes in many different varieties—sweet, dry, light, bold—so be sure to pick one that has a flavor you like.

2 ounces sake

1 ounce Skinnygirl Cucumber Vodka or other cucumber-flavored or unflavored vodka

½ ounce fresh lime juice

Cucumber spear, for garnish

Combine the sake, vodka, and lime juice in a cocktail shaker with ice and shake until well chilled. Strain into a chilled martini glass. Garnish with a spear of fresh cucumber.

pink lemon drop

This delightfully ladylike martini is my take on the classic lemon drop.

SERVES 2

6 to 8 fresh (or thawed frozen) raspberries

3 ounces Skinnygirl Meyer Lemon Vodka or other lemon-flavored vodka

1½ ounces Cointreau or other orange or citrus liqueur

3 ounces lemon Sour Mix (page 17)

Lemon wheel, for garnish

Muddle the raspberries in the bottom of a cocktail shaker. Add the vodka, Cointreau, sour mix, and ice. Shake well. Strain into a chilled martini glass. Garnish with a lemon wheel on the rim.

KEEP THE LIGHTS ON LOW

Nothing kills a party faster than overly bright lights. They're unflattering, and it makes people feel like they're at the office. Soft, low lighting makes everyone look better. So put your lights on dimmers, use lamps instead of overhead lights, and be sure to set out plenty of candles. Buy some simple tea light holders and spread them around to add a nice glow to the room—just be careful not to use scented candles if you're serving food or you'll have too many competing smells. For outdoor parties, votives placed in colored paper bags are cute. Lanterns, strings of white Christmas lights, and tiki torches are also nice ways to provide flattering light.

apple martini
*under 150 calories

A beautiful green appletini that is as fun to look at as it is to drink.

1¼ ounces vodka

½ ounce green apple schnapps, such as Pucker

1 ounce fresh lemon juice

½ ounce Simple Syrup (page 8)

Green apple slices, for garnish

Combine the vodka, apple schnapps, lemon juice, and simple syrup with ice in a cocktail shaker and shake well. Strain into a chilled martini glass. Garnish with apple slices.

VARIATIONS: You could also garnish with a piece of sour apple candy. If you want to turn this into a Caramel Apple Martini, drizzle the inside of the glass with sugar-free caramel sauce before you pour in the drink.

french kiss

My sweet and sexy twist on the classic Cosmopolitan, the flirtiest of all the martinis.

Two to four 1-inch chunks fresh pineapple

3 ounces Skinnygirl White Cherry Vodka or other cherry-flavored vodka

1½ ounces Chambord or other raspberry liqueur

Pineapple wedge, for garnish

Muddle the pineapple in a cocktail shaker. Add the vodka, Chambord, and some ice and shake well. Double-strain (using both the cocktail strainer and a small sieve) into a chilled martini glass. Garnish with a wedge of pineapple on the rim.

THE ICE BREAKER

You may be used to breaking the ice in conversation, but it's just as important to do when shaking your cocktails. You want to get them as cold as you possibly can. So once you've loaded up the cocktail shaker with your ingredients and plenty of ice, put the lid on and shake what your mama gave you. Keep at it for at least 15 seconds, until the ice cubes are broken up a bit and the drink is icy cold. Then pour your very cool cocktail into a chilled glass and drink it right away.

SEXY
SANGRIAS
&
SPRITZERS

"

I love wine, and I love cocktails. So what could be better than combining the two? These sangrias and spritzers are seriously refreshing. A wine punch that originated in Spain and Portugal, sangria is perfection in a pitcher and is always a hit with a crowd. Many sangria recipes are loaded down with sugar, but I like to keep mine fruity and light. Make it using red, white, or sparkling wine and whatever fruit is in season, and your fiesta will be off to a delicious start.

ravishing red sangria
*under 150 calories

This red sangrias is bold but has a perfect hint of sweetness, and it's nice even in cooler weather. It holds up in the fridge, so you can make it well ahead of time. Don't be afraid to mix it up and use other fruit too!

SERVES 6 TO 8

One 750 ml bottle Skinnygirl California Red or Cabernet Sauvignon, or other red wine

3 ounces vodka (optional)

2 ounces triple sec or other orange or citrus liqueur

2 ounces lemon Sour Mix (page 17)

2 ounces orange juice

1 orange, sliced

1 apple, sliced

A handful of green grapes, cut in half

Diet lemon-lime or club soda, for serving (optional)

1. Combine the wine, vodka (if using), triple sec, sour mix, and orange juice in a pitcher and stir. Refrigerate for at least an hour to chill well.

2. Before serving, drop in the orange, apple, and grapes. Add ice cubes (the larger, the better) to the pitcher. Serve over ice in a red wine glass. If you like your sangria on the lighter side, top it off with a splash of soda.

VARIATION: Use different fruits depending on the season. For winter, pears, grapefruits, and other citrus fruits are nice. In spring and summer, peaches, plums, and berries are perfect—though they're softer so they'll get mushy if they sit too long in liquid. Add them as closely as possible to when you're serving to keep them intact.

white sangria
*under 150 calories

White wine gives sangria a lighter, sweeter flavor that's perfect for warmer weather and daytime celebrations. It can also be made ahead of time and pairs well with almost any kind of fruit.

SERVES 6 TO 8

One 750 ml bottle Skinnygirl Moscato or other white wine

3 ounces vodka (optional)

3 ounces lemon Sour Mix (page 17)

3 ounces peach juice or nectar

2 or 3 fresh (or thawed frozen) peaches, nectarines, or plums, or a combination of all three, cut into thin slices

Diet lemon-lime or club soda, for serving (optional)

1. Combine the moscato, vodka (if using), sour mix, and peach juice in a pitcher and stir. Refrigerate for at least an hour to chill well.

2. Before serving, drop in the fruit slices. Add ice cubes (the larger, the better) to the pitcher. Serve over ice in white wine glasses. If you like your sangria on the lighter side, top it off with a splash of soda.

VARIATIONS: Go tropical by using pineapples, mangos, and strawberries. Make it extra summery by using assorted melons or berries. Or do an all-white sangria using white grapes and white peaches. With any of the more tender fruits, don't add them too far ahead of time or they'll get mushy.

pretty in pink sangria
*under 150 calories

Rosé gives this delicate sangria a beautiful shade of pink that perfectly complements any ladylike occasion.

SERVES 6 TO 8

One 750 ml bottle Skinnygirl California Rosé Blend or other rosé

3 ounces vodka (optional)

3 ounces lemon Sour Mix (page 17)

3 ounces strawberry or strawberry juice blend

1 lemon, sliced

3 or 4 fresh (or thawed frozen) strawberries, sliced

Diet lemon-lime or club soda, for serving (optional)

1. Combine the wine, vodka (if using), sour mix, and juice in a pitcher and stir. Refrigerate for at least an hour to chill well.

2. Before serving, add ice cubes (the larger, the better) to the pitcher and drop in the lemon and sliced strawberries. Serve over ice in white wine glasses. If you like your sangria on the lighter side, top it off with a splash of soda.

VARIATIONS: Change up the fruit by using other types of berries and citrus. Melons and peaches also go nicely with rosé. Just be careful not to let the fruit sit in the sangria for too long, or it will get mushy.

sassy sparkling sangria
*under 150 calories

This sangria is as fizzy and festive as it comes. Unlike its sturdier san-gria sisters, this one can't be made ahead of time because its bubbles will fall flat—so be sure to serve it immediately after you make it.

One 750 ml bottle Skinnygirl Prosecco or other sparkling wine

4 ounces Pink Grapefruit Skinnygirl Sparklers or diet lemon-lime or grapefruit soda

4 ounces club soda

1 peach, pitted and sliced

1 yellow plum, pitted and sliced

A handful of green grapes, cut in half

1. Put the prosecco and sodas in the fridge for at least an hour ahead of time, so they're well chilled.

2. Combine the prosecco and sodas in a pitcher and stir. Add ice cubes (the larger, the better) and the fruit. Serve over ice in a white wine glass.

VARIATIONS: This is extra pretty if you use a mix of fresh or frozen berries (pictured) instead of peaches and plums. Or you can do a mix of sliced lem-ons, limes, oranges, and grapefruit.

cucumber-lime spritzer

Whether you're making a glass for yourself or relaxing with your girls, this effervescent white wine cocktail is as cool as it gets.

1½ ounces Skinnygirl Cucumber Vodka or other cucumber-flavored
    vodka
Juice of ½ lime
4½ ounces Skinnygirl Prosecco or other sparkling wine
Lime twist, for garnish

Combine the vodka and lime juice with ice in a cocktail shaker and shake well. Strain into a chilled champagne flute. Top with the prosecco and garnish with a lime twist.

SPARKLING
COCKTAILS

❝❞

Sparkling cocktails are currently very on-trend, and old-fashioned Champagne cocktails are making a big comeback. And for good reason: they're chic, sexy, and fun to drink. Use my Skinnygirl Prosecco or any Champagne you love to mix up one of these flirty classics, but don't stop there! Try adding some sparkle to any vodka or gin cocktail you love and see where the night takes you.

french 75

Pretend you're a Parisian for the night and say oui to my version of the ultimate Champagne cocktail!

1½ ounces gin or vodka

1½ ounces lemon Sour Mix (page 17)

4½ ounces Skinnygirl Prosecco or Champagne

Lemon twist, for garnish

Combine the gin and sour mix with ice in a cocktail shaker and shake well. Strain into a chilled champagne flute. Top it off with the prosecco and garnish with a lemon twist.

TWIST AND SHOUT

A twist adds a touch of class to any drink. Lemon twists are the most common, but you can also use oranges and limes. Start by cutting a wheel of lemon. Slice the wheel almost in half, but don't cut through the peel on the opposite side. Carefully slice the fruit and white pith away from the peel. You should be left with one long strip of peel. Twist it into a spiral and hold it there for a second. Voilà! You've got a twist. Add extra lemon flavor to your drink by running the colored side of the twist along the rim of the glass before using it as the garnish.

kir royale

This French delight is as lovely for brunch as it is in the evening.

1 ounce crème de cassis or other black currant– or berry-flavored
   liqueur

5 ounces Skinnygirl Prosecco

Lemon twist, for garnish

Pour the crème de cassis into a champagne flute, then pour the prosecco on top. Garnish with a lemon twist.

skinnygirl snacks

Snack Talkin'

Store-bought goodies are a great way to make things easier for yourself, so you don't have to stress about making all the food from scratch—the key is knowing what to buy. I like to choose foods that people can easily serve themselves and that don't go bad if they get cold.

Healthy finger foods like edamame, spiced nuts, wasabi peas, and sliced-up vegetables are perfect go-tos for any theme. Dumplings or the yummy empanadas from Trader Joe's are great, too. It's nice to put your own twist on things, so instead of serving plain hummus, doctor it up with some herbs or spices. My line of Skinnygirl hummus comes in a variety of flavors like Roasted Red Pepper and Cilantro Jalapeño, so all you need to do is add a garnish and you have a perfect party dip. Or put out sushi on a nice platter and serve it with a dipping sauce that you've floated sesame seeds on. Make your own version of mixed nuts and add some herbs or spices to give them a little extra punch.

One of my favorite things to do is to make a big antipasto platter: Put olives and a few different marinated veggies in ramekins or other small bowls. (You can buy these inexpensively at IKEA.) Lay out the ramekins with a selection of meats and cheeses on a nice cutting board—it ends up looking really gourmet.

Whatever you do, the most important rule is never to serve anything in the bag or jar that it came in. Even if you're not doctoring up something, take a minute to put what you've bought on pretty plates or in good bowls that fit the theme. Even microwave popcorn can look gourmet if it's in a fancy bowl. If I'm pressed for time, I'll quickly pop some Skinnygirl popcorn in my favorite Lime and Salt flavor (yum!) and put it in a festive bowl before my guests walk through the door. If you take the time to make food look nice, no one will ever notice or care that it came from the supermarket.

prosecco with raspberries

*under 150 calories

The berries add a beautiful red color to the bubbly and make it into something really special.

4 or 5 fresh (or thawed frozen) raspberries

1 teaspoon raw sugar

6 ounces chilled Skinnygirl Prosecco, other sparkling wine, or Champagne

In a small bowl, muddle the raspberries with the sugar. Pour or spoon the mixture into a champagne flute. Top it off with the prosecco.

red carpet royale

*under 150 calories

Be the star of any party with this elegant cocktail.

2 ounces Skinnygirl Prosecco or Champagne

1 ounce Skinnygirl White Cherry Vodka or other cherry-flavored vodka

Frozen cherry, for garnish

Pour the prosecco into a champagne flute and top with the vodka. Garnish with a frozen cherry.

BERRY FANCY

Frozen berries are a great way to add a little flair to almost any drink. You can, of course, buy frozen berries by the bag. But I like to freeze any berries I have that are slightly overripe, so I can use them in my cocktails later. Dropping a frozen blueberry or blackberry into a vodka drink will turn it a gorgeous shade of light purple. Raspberries and strawberries give a lovely pinkish hue—and they're also a great way to keep a glass of Champagne extra cold. You can also class up your ice cubes by freezing berries inside them. To do that, simply place a berry in each cube of your ice cube tray, add water, and then freeze.

bellini

*under 150 calories

Nothing beats the crisp sweetness of a Bellini at brunch.

½ ounce white peach puree

4 ounces Skinnygirl Prosecco or other sparkling wine, chilled

Splash of lemon Sour Mix (page 17)

Spoon the white peach puree into the bottom of a champagne flute. Top with the prosecco and sour mix.

VARIATION: This is great with other fruits, too. Blood oranges, mangos, and raspberries all work wonderfully. You can make your own puree by muddling or blending whatever fruit you like—just be sure to remove any pits or peels before you blend and strain the puree before using it.

TROPICAL
PARADISE

66 99

Picture yourself sitting on a gorgeous beach, sipping a giant rum cocktail with a cute little umbrella in it. It's the ultimate fantasy, but don't let the usual high-calorie island cocktails ruin it. Instead, live the dream with these Skinnygirl tropical treats. They are as fruity and fabulous as the originals, but totally guilt-free.

polynesian punch

*under 150 calories

Get ready to be transported to your own little tropical island with this grown-up version of Hawaiian Punch.

1¼ ounces light rum

2 ounces passion fruit juice

1 ounce pineapple juice

½ ounce cranberry juice

Pineapple wedge, for garnish

Combine the rum and juices over ice in a hurricane glass. Garnish with a wedge of pineapple on the rim.

mai tai
*under 150 calories

I normally advise against drinking dark liquor, but here is one place where you might want to bend the rules. Dark rum gives this drink its wonderful flavor and lends a bit of color, too, so I give you my blessing to go for it!

1¼ ounces aged dark rum (light rum is fine, too)

½ ounce orange curaçao or other orange or citrus liqueur

Juice of 1 lime (reserve one half of the lime after juicing it, for garnish)

½ ounce sugar-free almond syrup (orgeat)*

Fresh mint sprig, for garnish

Cherry, for garnish

Combine the rum, orange curaçao, lime juice, and almond syrup with ice in a cocktail shaker and shake well. Strain over fresh crushed ice in a hurricane or goblet glass. Garnish with a mint sprig, the spent lime shell, and a cherry—this is a cute way to represent a palm tree, island, and the setting sun.

*You can buy this at Target and many grocery stores.

tiki punch

*under 150 calories

Get in the island spirit with this juicy crowd-pleaser.

2 fresh strawberries, sliced

1¼ ounces light rum

1 ounce orange juice

1 ounce mango juice

Orange half-wheel, for garnish

Freshly grated nutmeg,
for garnish

Muddle the strawberries in the bottom of a cocktail shaker. Add the rum, orange juice, and mango juice, along with ice. Shake well. Double-strain (using both the cocktail strainer and a small sieve) over fresh ice in a tiki glass. (A hurricane glass or goblet would work, too.) Garnish with a half-wheel of orange. You can also add a dusting of nutmeg on top, if you like.

blue hawaiian

This shockingly blue drink is tons of fun, and it's guaranteed to electrify your next backyard luau.

¾ ounce light rum

¾ ounce vodka

½ ounce blue curaçao

3 ounces pineapple juice

1½ ounces lemon Sour Mix
(page 17)

Pineapple wedge, for garnish

Combine the rum, vodka, blue curaçao, pineapple juice, and sour mix in a cocktail shaker with ice and shake until well chilled. Strain over fresh ice in a hurricane glass. Garnish with a pineapple wedge on the rim speared with a cocktail umbrella.

VARIATION: To make this a frozen drink, fill the glass you're serving it in with ice, then dump the ice into a blender. Add the rest of the ingredients and blend until smooth. Pour into the glass and garnish.

the rum runner

This gorgeous frozen cocktail is like holding a tropical sunset in your hand.

1 ounce light rum

1 ounce Cruzan Banana Rum or other banana liqueur

¾ ounce blackberry brandy or berry liqueur

2 ounces low-calorie orange juice

¼ ounce Monin sugar-free pomegranate syrup

Pineapple wedge, for garnish

Cherry, for garnish

Fill the glass you're serving the drink in with ice, then dump the ice into a blender. Add the light rum, banana rum, brandy, juice, and syrup and blend until smooth. Pour into the glass. Garnish with a pineapple wedge and a cherry on the rim.

hurricane

A breezy concoction that will blow you away with its deliciousness.

1½ ounces light rum

1½ ounces low-calorie orange juice

1½ ounces passion fruit juice

Juice of ½ lime

½ ounce Monin sugar-free pomegranate syrup*

Orange half-wheel, for garnish

Lime wheel, for garnish

Combine the rum, juices, and syrup with ice in a cocktail shaker and shake well. Strain over fresh ice in a hurricane glass. Garnish with a half-wheel of orange and a lime wheel.

*If you can't find this, use grenadine instead—but just be aware that it will add 45 calories to the drink.

the tiki torch

This super fruity and flavorful cocktail is a bit of paradise in a glass.

1½ ounces Skinnygirl White Cherry Vodka or other cherry-flavored
   vodka

3 ounces apricot juice or nectar

1½ ounces mango-lemonade

½ ounce almond-flavored syrup (orgeat)

Fresh mint sprig, for garnish

Freshly grated nutmeg, for garnish

Combine the vodka, apricot juice, lemonade, and syrup with crushed ice in a cocktail shaker and shake well. Pour into a hurricane glass. Garnish with a mint sprig and a dusting of nutmeg.

inspired infusions

Infused vodkas look fancy, but they're actually an amazingly easy way to add another layer of flavor to your cocktails. Start with plain vodka (clear tequila and rum also work) and add any combination of herbs, spices, vegetables, or fruits that sounds good. I love using jalapeños to bring the heat. Fruits like pineapples, citrus, and berries are lovely. Vanilla beans and cinnamon sticks are great for warming up a cold-weather cocktail.

To make infusions, combine your ingredients (slice up anything large into smaller chunks) with the liquor in an airtight container. Let them steep in a cool, dark place. Super spicy things like chiles only need a few hours. But mellower flavors need anywhere from a few days to two weeks to infuse—just taste the vodka occasionally until it is as strong as you want it. Then strain it into a new container and use it to mix up your favorite cocktail.

Here are some of my favorite combinations to get you started:

- Tequila with jalapeño chiles

- Tequila with chipotle chiles

- Tequila with dried chiles

- Vodka with watermelon

- Vodka with pineapple

- Vodka with lemons, limes, or oranges

- Vodka with mixed fresh berries

- Rum with cinnamon sticks

- Rum with blood oranges and vanilla beans

A 1.5-ounce portion of any of these has under 150 calories.

SPICY &
SEXY

"

Go to any hip mixology bar and you'll see lots of spiced-up cocktails on the menu. Pairing chiles with fruit is very trendy right now, and it's a great way to make drinks that are both really hot and very cool. It's also an ideal way to pack a lot of flavor punch into a drink without adding tons of extra calories. Don't be afraid to bring the heat home with these saucy little numbers.

blue mexico

This gorgeous drink is a little bit peppery and a little bit sweet.

6 fresh (or thawed frozen) blueberries, plus a few extra for garnish

1-inch slice yellow bell pepper, coarsely chopped

1¼ ounces white (clear) tequila (100% agave)

½ ounce triple sec or other orange or citrus liqueur

2 ounces lemon Sour Mix (page 17)

Lemon wheel, for garnish

Muddle the blueberries and bell pepper in the bottom of a cocktail shaker. Add the tequila, triple sec, and sour mix and shake with ice until well chilled. Double-strain (using both the cocktail strainer and a small sieve) into a chilled martini glass. Garnish with a lemon wheel and blueberries.

hot mango

A seductive cocktail that is just fiery enough to be dangerous.

1¼ ounces reposado tequila (100% agave; this is a top-shelf tequila, but you can use any clear tequila)

½ ounce triple sec or other orange or citrus liqueur

1½ ounces lemon Sour Mix (page 17)

1 ounce mango nectar or juice

A few dashes of Tabasco sauce*

Lime half-wheel, for garnish

Combine the tequila, triple sec, sour mix, mango nectar, and Tabasco in a cocktail shaker with ice and shake until well blended. Strain into a chilled martini glass and garnish with a lime half-wheel on the rim.

*Instead of using Tabasco, you could muddle the chile of your choice in the cocktail shaker before adding the rest of the ingredients. If you do this, be sure to double-strain the drink (using both the cocktail strainer and a small sieve) to get out any seeds or bits of chile.

smoky maria
*under 150 calories

This smoldering version of the Bloody Mary isn't just for brunch—it's strong enough to go all night long.

1½ ounces white (clear) tequila (100% agave) or vodka

1 canned chipotle chile

3 to 4 ounces Bloody Mary mix*

Lemon wedge, for garnish

Lime wedge, for garnish

Combine the tequila, chipotle, and Bloody Mary mix with ice in a pint serving glass. Pour it back and forth between the serving glass and a mixing glass until well mixed. Garnish with lemon and lime wedges on the rim.

*You can buy Bloody Mary mix or make your own by combining the following ingredients in a blender: 4 ounces tomato juice, 4 to 6 dashes of Worchester sauce, 3 to 5 dashes Tabasco sauce, 3 to 5 grinds of fresh pepper, 3 dashes onion salt, 3 dashes garlic salt, and 3 fresh basil leaves (torn into pieces). Refrigerate for at least 2 hours, or preferably overnight, before using.

chipotle margarita

A fiery but refreshing take on the margarita.

1¼ ounces tequila infused with chipotle chile (see page 69)

½ ounce triple sec or other orange or citrus liqueur

2 ounces lime Sour Mix (page 17)

Splash of fresh lime juice

Strip of orange peel or candied orange peel, for garnish (see below)

Combine the tequila, triple sec, sour mix, and lime juice with ice in a cocktail shaker and shake until well chilled. Strain over fresh ice in a margarita or pint glass. Garnish by dropping in a strip of orange peel.

GORGEOUS GARNISHES

Candied citrus peels look beautiful, and they make a great garnish for almost any cocktail. They're easy to make, and keep for a while, so you can have them around to class up a drink anytime.

To make them, use a vegetable peeler to remove thin strips of peel from a navel orange or a lemon. Place the peels in a saucepan and add enough cold water to cover them by 2 inches. Bring the water to a boil, then drain the water from the peels. Again cover them with cold water, bring to a boil, and drain. Repeat this 4 times. (This removes the bitterness.) On the last boil, add 1 to 2 cups of sugar to the water and simmer for 10 minutes. Drain the peels and dip them in dry sugar to coat them. Arrange them in a single layer on a nonstick mat on a baking sheet and bake at a very low temperature (about 200° to 250°F) until the peels are glazed, about an hour. Allow them to cool and dry on the mat, then store at room temperature in a resealable plastic container of sugar.

SUMMER
FAVORITES

66 99

Summer is packed with chances to party, and when it's hot outside everyone wants to cool off with a cocktail. Whether you and your girls are lounging poolside or you're hosting a big barbecue, these warm-weather favorites are the perfect way to stay fresh while getting frisky. They're all bursting with fruity flavor but are still light enough to ensure you'll fit in your sexiest bikini and be ready to hit the beach the next day.

mango tango

*under 150 calories

Fun and fruity, this is a fabulous way to stay cool on a steamy day.

1½ ounces Skinnygirl Meyer Lemon Vodka or other citrus-flavored
   vodka

3 ounces mango juice or mango juice blend

1½ ounces Skinnygirl Sparklers Tangerine Mango or low-calorie orange
   soda or club soda

Lemon half-wheel, for garnish

Lime half-wheel, for garnish

Combine the vodka, juice, and soda over ice in a tall (highball) glass. Stir until
mixed. Garnish with half-wheels of lemon and lime on the rim.

the mojito
*under 150 calories

Mojitos are usually made with mixes that have a lot of sugar, but my version is light and won't make you feel like you just drank your dessert. If you're not in the mood for muddling, my Ready-to-Drink Skinnygirl Mojitos are always an option.

8 to 12 fresh mint leaves

1 ounce Simple Syrup (page 8), honey, or agave nectar

Juice of 1 lime

1½ ounces light rum or vodka

1 to 2 ounces club soda

Fresh mint sprig, for garnish

Lime wedge, for garnish

Place the mint leaves in the bottom of a tall (highball) glass and top with the simple syrup and lime juice. Muddle with a pestle or long spoon until the mint is fragrant but not torn. Fill the glass with ice and add the rum. Stir until the mint leaves pull up through the cocktail. Top off with club soda and stir again. Garnish with a mint sprig and a lime wedge.

VARIATIONS: Use cucumber-flavored vodka or gin and garnish with a cucumber slice. Use tangerine- or orange-flavored vodka and garnish with an orange wheel.

tangerine dream

*under 150 calories

Pucker up to this cool citrus-y concoction.

1½ ounces Skinnygirl Tangerine Vodka or other citrus-flavored vodka

3 ounces lemon Sour Mix (page 17)

Splash of orange juice

Orange wheel, for garnish

Cherry, for garnish

Combine the vodka, sour mix, and orange juice over ice in a tall (highball) glass. Stir until mixed. Use a toothpick to make an orange and cherry flag for garnish.

the cherry blossom

*under 150 calories

This pretty cocktail is a delicate bouquet of pink bubbles.

1½ ounces Skinnygirl White Cherry Vodka or other cherry-flavored
vodka

3 ounces cranberry-cherry juice drink

1½ ounces Skinnygirl Sparklers Pink Grapefruit or other low-calorie
citrus soda

Lime wedge, for garnish

Combine the vodka, juice, and soda over ice in a tall (highball) glass. Garnish
with a lime wedge on the rim.

STOP STAINS IN THEIR TRACKS

First of all, if you have a white carpet or white furniture, never
serve anything red. It's just not worth it! Whenever possible, use
white grape juice or white cranberry juice if you have carpets.
Your best defense against stains is to be prepared. Put out coasters everywhere. This will protect your furniture and cut down on
post-party stickiness, too. Keep a stain remover stick handy, too,
for quick clothing clean-ups. If a spill happens, act quickly to dab
up the stain—never rub a stain on carpet!—as much as you can
with water or club soda and a rag. Then apply some soapy water
or a stain remover you trust. (I prefer some dish soap in water
because some products can really screw up your carpet.) Never
wait until after the party is over to clean up a stain; that will only
make the job harder.

sex on the beach

Who could resist a Skinnygirl version of the most titillating cocktail of all?

1 ounce Skinnygirl White Cherry Vodka or other cherry-flavored vodka

1 ounce Skinnygirl Tangerine Vodka or other citrus-flavored vodka

1½ ounces orange juice

1½ ounces cranberry juice

Splash of peach schnapps

Splash of crème de cassis or other black currant– or berry-flavored
liqueur

Orange half-wheel, for garnish

Cherry, for garnish

Combine the vodkas, juices, schnapps, and crème de cassis with ice in a cocktail shaker and shake well. Strain over fresh ice in a tall (highball) glass. Garnish with an orange half-wheel on the rim and a cherry dropped in.

the bathing beauty

This is a sweeter twist on the Sea Breeze, a classic poolside cocktail that's normally made with cranberry and grapefruit juice. If pineapple is not your thing, you can substitute almost any other kind of fruit juice that appeals to you.

1½ ounces vodka

3 ounces pineapple juice

Large splash of low-calorie cranberry juice

Pineapple wedge, for garnish

Combine the vodka and juices over ice in a tall (highball) glass. Stir until mixed. Garnish with a wedge of pineapple on the rim.

lemon-melon tongue twister

*under 150 calories

This delightful watermelon-y mouthful will keep you looking fresh while you're basking sexily on your beach towel.

1½ ounces Skinnygirl Meyer Lemon Vodka or other lemon-flavored vodka

3 ounces watermelon juice*

1½ ounces limeade

Fresh mint sprig, for garnish

Watermelon wedge, for garnish

Combine the vodka and juices over ice in a tall (highball) glass. Stir until mixed. Garnish with a mint sprig and a watermelon wedge on the rim.

*You can buy this or you can make your own juice by cutting up fresh watermelon and putting it in the blender. Take out as many seeds as you can before you blend it. Pour it through a fine-mesh strainer when you're done to remove the pulp and remaining seeds.

tina collins

*under 150 calories

This light and lemony summer classic makes a great afternoon refreshment.

1½ ounces gin or Skinnygirl Meyer Lemon Vodka

3 ounces lemon Sour Mix (page 17)

1½ ounces club soda

Lime wedge, for garnish

Cherry, for garnish

Combine the gin, sour mix, and club soda over ice in a tall (highball) glass. Stir until mixed. Garnish with a lime wedge and a cherry.

┌─ PRO PARTY TIP ─────────────────────────────

If you're looking to add extra decor to a party, set out some nice glass vases filled with lemons and limes. They look elegant, and they're also secretly useful! If you start to run short of garnishes, you can always grab a lemon or lime from the vase and slice it up.

the nude boy
*under 150 calories

Perfect for sipping on a hot day, this cocktail is light and refreshing with just a hint of cucumber and pomegranate.

1½ ounces Skinnygirl Cucumber Vodka or other cucumber-flavored vodka

3 ounces club soda

Splash of pomegranate juice

Lemon wheel, for garnish

Combine the vodka and club soda over ice in a tall (highball) glass. Stir to combine. Pour on a splash of pomegranate juice to top it off. Float the lemon wheel on top.

IF YOU'RE DRINKING, YOU'RE NOT DRIVING

The most important part of any party is making sure your guests get home safely. If you're sober, offer rides home to guests in need, and don't hesitate to call someone a cab. It's not a big inconvenience—there are even services that will come pick up their car for them the next morning—and it could be a real lifesaver. And, of course, if you're out on the town, designate a driver to make sure everyone in your group gets home safe and sound.

CULINARY
COCKTAILS

" "

Fresh herbs like mint, basil, thyme, sage, cilantro, and rosemary are popping up on cocktail menus everywhere. You can use them to infuse alcohol (see page 69), but for a stronger punch add them right into the drink. Use these delicious recipes as your guide and experiment to find your favorite flavors. No matter how you incorporate the herbs, always save a few sprigs to use as an eye-catching garnish.

strawberry basil burst

*under 150 calories

Basil goes particularly well with berries and adds an extra level of special to this beautiful drink.

2 large fresh (or thawed frozen) strawberries, sliced (reserve 2 slices for garnish)

2 fresh basil leaves, torn, plus 1 whole leaf for garnish

1½ ounces vodka

1½ ounces lemon Sour Mix (page 17)

Splash of club soda

Muddle the strawberries and basil in the bottom of a cocktail shaker. Add the vodka, sour mix, and ice and shake until well chilled. Double-strain (using both the cocktail strainer and a small sieve) over fresh ice in a tall (highball) glass. Top it off with club soda and garnish with the remaining strawberry slices and the basil leaf.

VARIATION: For an unusual but delicious garnish, grind some fresh pepper on top of the drink.

the good thyme girl
*under 150 calories

This herby, cooling tonic will bring some much-needed serenity to even the craziest day.

1½ ounces Skinnygirl Cucumber Vodka or other cucumber-flavored vodka

1½ ounces lemonade

1½ ounces watermelon juice

Leaves stripped from a 2-inch sprig of fresh thyme, plus a small sprig for garnish

Fresh watermelon ball, for garnish

Combine the vodka, lemonade, juice, and thyme leaves with ice in a cocktail shaker and shake until well chilled. Double-strain (using both the cocktail strainer and a small sieve) into a chilled martini glass. Garnish on the rim with the thyme sprig speared into the watermelon ball.

spicy latina
*under 150 calories

A sexy, cilantro-packed cocktail that will add a little fire to any fiesta.

⅓-inch slice jalapeño chile or 2 to 3 dashes of green Tabasco sauce

Three ½-inch slices peeled cucumber

¼ cup fresh cilantro leaves (15 to 20 leaves; reserve 1 leaf for garnish)

1½ ounces white (clear) tequila (100% agave)

1 ounce fresh lemon or lime juice

½ ounce Simple Syrup (page 8)

Lime wheel, for garnish

Muddle the jalapeño in the bottom of a cocktail shaker. Add the cucumber and cilantro and muddle again. Add the tequila, juice, and simple syrup and shake with ice until well chilled. Double-strain (using both the cocktail strainer and a small sieve) into a chilled martini glass. Garnish with a lime wheel on the rim and float a cilantro leaf on top.

pretty pear

*under 150 calories

The rosemary adds a subtle edge to the sweetness of the pear in this light and lovely cocktail.

3-inch sprig of fresh rosemary

1 canned pear half (in light syrup), drained (or you can use pear puree)

1½ ounces light rum

1 ounce fresh lemon juice

Lemon wheel, for garnish

Strip the bottom inch of leaves from the rosemary sprig and reserve the sprig for garnish. Chop the rosemary leaves and put them in a cocktail shaker. Add the pear half and muddle. Add the rum and lemon juice and shake with ice until well chilled. Double-strain (using both the cocktail strainer and a small sieve) into a chilled martini glass. Garnish on the rim with the rosemary sprig and a lemon wheel.

watermelon & basil margarita

Cool off with this classed-up culinary version of a margarita.

Four 1-inch cubes seedless watermelon

2 fresh basil leaves, torn into pieces

1¼ ounces white (clear) tequila (100% agave)

½ ounce triple sec or other orange or citrus liqueur

2 ounces lemon Sour Mix (page 17)

Juice of ½ lime

Watermelon spear, for garnish

Muddle the watermelon cubes and basil leaves in the bottom of a cocktail shaker. Add the tequila, triple sec, sour mix, and lime juice and shake with ice until well chilled. Double-strain (using both the cocktail strainer and a small sieve) over fresh ice in a margarita or pint glass. Garnish with a watermelon spear on the rim.

skinnygirl snacks

Bruschetta is a perfect party food—it's simple, it's elegant, and it's delicious. I love this classic recipe, but you can also make it using whatever ingredients you like.

bruschetta with tomatoes and fresh basil

SERVES 2

6 thin slices whole-grain French baguette or Italian bread

1 clove garlic

1 tablespoon plus 1 teaspoon olive oil

3 plum tomatoes, chopped

1 tablespoon chopped fresh basil

1 teaspoon balsamic vinegar

Salt and pepper

1. Preheat the oven to 450°F.

2. Arrange the bread slices on a baking sheet. Bake for 5 to 6 minutes, until the bread looks lightly toasted.

3. Cut the garlic in half and rub the cut sides on each slice of bread. Drizzle the bread with 1 tablespoon of the olive oil.

4. Toss the tomatoes, basil, balsamic vinegar, and remaining olive oil in a bowl. Divide this mixture between the bread slices, heaping it on top. Season with salt and pepper. Serve immediately.

VARIATIONS: You can take this basic idea and make these with almost any topping you want. I love to do sautéed mushrooms with pecorino cheese, drizzled with truffle oil. Roasted butternut squash is nice with a little ricotta or goat cheese, topped with fresh sage. If you want to add meat, prosciutto works well with cantaloupe and a little balsamic vinegar.

FROZEN

FANTASIES

"

There's almost nothing that's harder to resist than the frosty charms of a frozen cocktail. Now you can skip the sticky mess of calories you'd get from most frozen drink mixes and indulge all you want. These lower-calorie versions of your icy favorites are pure pleasure—with none of the guilt! Whip up these satisfying chillers while hanging with friends on a steamy summer night or whenever a craving for something cool strikes.

frozen piña colada

Piña coladas are one of my favorites, but they often have a whopping 500 calories. Luckily, my version—which is also part of my Ready-to-Drink cocktail line—is far better for you but tastes just as indulgent.

1½ ounces light rum

3 ounces coconut milk or light coconut milk

2 tablespoons crushed pineapple, drained

Pineapple wedge, for garnish

Combine the rum, coconut milk, and pineapple in a blender with ice. Blend until smooth. Pour into a hurricane glass. Garnish with a pineapple wedge on the rim.

A HINT OF SWEETNESS

If you like your cocktails a little sweeter but are afraid of pouring on the calories, try my Skinnygirl liquid sweeteners. One squeeze of my stevia sweetener has the same sweetness as a teaspoon of sugar but has zero calories and is made with natural ingredients. This makes it a great alternative to the simple syrup recipe at the beginning of this book. I keep the tiny bottle in my purse and use it to sweeten everything—iced tea, Greek yogurt, or cocktails at a party!

mudslide

The ultimate in frozen decadence—this is like a chocolate milkshake, only better!

1 ounce vodka

1 ounce coffee liqueur

One 2-ounce scoop low-calorie vanilla frozen yogurt

Chocolate curls, for garnish*

Combine the vodka, coffee liqueur, and frozen yogurt with ice in a blender and blend until smooth. Pour into a coupe glass. Garnish with chocolate curls.

*You can shave these off a block of chocolate, using a vegetable peeler.

frozen banana daiquiri

This satisfyingly rich beauty is so delicious it'll drive you bananas!

1½ ounces light rum

1 banana, peeled
(optional: reserve a 2-inch
piece from one end for garnish)

Juice of ½ lime

Lime wheel, for garnish

Combine the rum, banana, and lime juice with ice in a blender. Blend until smooth. Pour into a coupe glass. Garnish with a lime wheel and/or the reserved piece of banana, if you like.

VARIATION: Make this a Frozen Strawberry Daiquiri by using 3 ounces strawberry puree instead of banana and the juice of a whole lime instead of a half. To make strawberry puree, you need 2 pounds frozen whole strawberries, thawed, and 1/2 cup Simple Syrup (page 8). Blend until smooth. You can freeze whatever you don't use right away.

skinnygirl snacks

For a summer party, you can't go wrong with this adorable and easy-to-make boozy dessert.

lemon sorbet in lemon peels

SERVES 4

4 lemons

1 to 2 pints lemon sorbet

4 shots Skinnygirl Meyer Lemon Vodka or other citrus-flavored vodka

4 fresh mint sprigs, for garnish

1. Cut off the top third of each lemon and reserve for the garnish. Hollow out the lemons and freeze the empty shells for 1 hour minimum, preferably overnight.

2. The next day, let the sorbet soften to the point that you can stir it a bit. Add the vodka to the sorbet and mix it until just combined. Fill each of the shells with the sorbet, cover, and refreeze them. (You can make these up to three days ahead of time. Just keep them covered and frozen.)

3. Before serving, garnish with a mint sprig and top with the reserved top of the lemon shell.

miami vice

This combo has a big wow factor and is a tasty way to show off two great cocktails in one gorgeous glass.

SERVES 2

1 serving of Frozen Strawberry Daiquiri (page 114)

1 serving of Frozen Piña Colada (page 113)

2 star fruit slices, for garnish

2 whole fresh strawberries, for garnish

2 pineapple wedges, for garnish

Pour the strawberry daiquiri into two hurricane glasses or pint glasses. Top with the piña colada so that you end up with a layered drink. Garnish with a pineapple wedge, strawberry, and star fruit slice on the rim.

AFTER-DINNER
DECADENCE

"

An after-dinner drink is the best of both worlds: a sexy cocktail and a dreamy dessert all in one. After a satisfying meal, a little something sweet is what you crave—but what you don't want is to pour a glass full of a sickly sweet liqueur. That's why I've put my Skinnygirl spin on these decadent delights. They're lower in calories but big on the fabulous rich flavor and sweetness you want after a delicious dinner.

death by chocolate

A sultry chocolate martini with a little kick, this is as seductive as it gets.

1 ounce vodka

1 ounce Godiva Chocolate Liqueur or Mocha Liqueur

1 ounce brewed espresso, room temperature

Chocolate sauce, for garnish

Combine the vodka, liqueur, and espresso in a shaker filled with ice. Rim a martini glass by dipping it in chocolate sauce, and pour a teaspoonful of chocolate sauce into the bottom of the glass. Shake the drink until well chilled and strain it into the glass.

cotton candy cosmo

A sweet little drink that makes a big splash when you serve it.

1½ ounces vodka

1 ounce cranberry or pomegranate juice

½ ounce crème de cassis or Chambord (any red or pink fruit liqueur will
work)

Small handful of pink cotton candy

Splash of club soda (optional)

Combine the vodka, juice, and liqueur with ice in a cocktail shaker and
shake until well chilled. You can either strain the drink into a chilled martini
glass over the cotton candy, or strain the drink into the glass first and float
the cotton candy on top. Top off with soda, if you like.

kiss me i'm irish
*under 150 calories

Who'd want a plain old coffee after dinner when you can have this rich and creamy delight?

4 ounces hot brewed coffee

½ ounce Baileys or other Irish cream liqueur

½ ounce dark crème de cacao or other dark chocolate liqueur

Nonfat whipped cream, for garnish

Chocolate curls, for garnish*

Combine the coffee and liqueurs in a coffee mug. If you like, layer some nonfat whipped cream on top and sprinkle on some chocolate curls.

*You can shave these off a block of chocolate, using a vegetable peeler.

skinnygirl snacks

This is a quick way to make a sweet treat that both kids and grownups will love. The variations are endless, since you can choose any cookie and ice cream flavor options you like—and you can even roll the sandwiches in your favorite ice cream topping to add another layer of fun.

easy ice cream sandwiches

MAKES 4 SERVINGS

1 pint nonfat or low-fat ice cream, any flavor

8 low-fat, low-calorie cookies, any kind (they just need to be big enough to hold a scoop of ice cream)

Sprinkles, candy, crushed nuts, or other ice cream toppings (optional)

1. Let the ice cream soften a bit at room temperature.

2. Put a scoop of ice cream on top of one of the cookies. Smooth out the ice cream with a spatula so that it covers the whole cookie. Put another cookie on top to make a sandwich. If you like, roll the sides of the sandwich in whatever topping you want. Lay the sandwich on a small baking sheet.

3. Make the other 3 sandwiches the same way. Wrap in plastic to mold. Place them in the freezer until the ice cream is completely firm.

4. Arrange and serve on a cake platter.

the sexy russian

You can't say nyet to this slimmed-down version of a White Russian.

1½ ounces vodka

1½ ounces Kahlúa or other coffee liqueur

3 ounces skim milk, 2% milk, or soy or almond milk

Combine the vodka, coffee liqueur, and milk with ice in a cocktail shaker and shake well. Strain over fresh ice in a rocks glass.

PARTY PREDICAMENTS

What to do if somebody gets too drunk?

If you're worried about people overindulging, start the party by taking people's keys. If someone does too much, the best thing to do is to take them into another room where you won't embarrass them and say, "You probably just didn't realize how strong the drinks were, but you are out of control. Either you need to go lie down, or I will call you a taxi. Your choice." Make them stay still in one spot until they can walk, then get them home. If they turn nasty, get your partner or a friend to help you get the drunk person out of the house and home safely—because you don't want to be liable for anything bad that happens.

pink panther

There is nothing girlier than this glass of pink perfection, complete with a red licorice straw.

1 ounce light rum

½ ounce strawberry liqueur

2 ounces pineapple juice

Splash of grenadine

Diet lemon-lime soda, as needed

Fresh strawberry, for garnish

Red licorice twist, for garnish

Pour the rum, liqueur, juice, and grenadine, in order, over ice in a tall (high-ball) glass. Top off with soda to fill the glass. Garnish with a strawberry on the rim and a red licorice twist.

CANDY CRUSH

Candy garnishes aren't just for dessert drinks. You can add one to any cocktail for a little touch of fun and sweetness. Be cheeky and float a gummy worm in a colorful martini. Add chocolate-covered nuts to a cocktail with a nutty liqueur or sprinkle chocolate-covered coffee beans on an espresso cocktail. Crush up some of your favorite hard candy and use it to garnish the rim of your next margarita.

MARK THE
OCCASION

66 99

I never need a reason to throw a party, but sometimes there's an occasion that you really want to celebrate in style. A signature cocktail is the perfect way to set the mood for any kind of affair—whether it's something simple like brunch with your besties or a more elaborate bash like an elegant engagement party. These tasty but trustworthy drinks will give you plenty of choices to start your next shindig off right.

cherry cola

*under 150 calories

This peppy little cocktail is perfect for your next PJ party with the girls—the cola will keep the gossip flowing all night long!

1½ ounces Skinnygirl White Cherry Vodka or other cherry-flavored
    vodka

3 ounces diet cola

Maraschino cherries, for garnish

Combine the vodka and cola over ice in a rocks glass. Stir until mixed. Garnish with cherries.

razz-beery

Beer is the classic go-to for game day, but did you know it also makes a very refreshing cocktail? Bring your A game on Superbowl Sunday with this unbeatable cocktail.

1 ounce vodka

1 ounce chilled light beer

2 ounces raspberry lemonade concentrate

2-3 fresh raspberries, for garnish

Lemon half-wedge, for garnish

Combine the vodka, beer, and lemonade concentrate with ice in a cocktail shaker and shake well. Strain into a chilled martini glass. Garnish with whole raspberries on a pick and a lemon half-wedge.

tickle me pink
*under 150 calories

Whether you're spending Valentine's Day with your special someone or bonding with all your single ladies, one thing's for sure: you're going to want a drink—and the more pink and sparkly it is, the better!

1 ounce Skinnygirl White Cherry Vodka or other cherry-flavored vodka

4 ounces sparkling water

Splash of pomegranate juice

Maraschino cherry, for garnish

Combine the vodka and sparkling water over ice in a tall (highball) glass. Stir until mixed. Add a splash of pomegranate juice. Garnish by dropping in a cherry.

BANISH BAD BREATH

Cocktails may taste good, but they can make your breath smell pretty foul. Here are a few ways to avoid scaring away your date with a case of dragon breath.

- Stick to clear alcohols and avoid overly sugary drinks, which is always a good idea anyway.
- Go for the garnishes: chew on a lemon or lime wedge or some mint leaves to give your breath a boost.
- Drink plenty of water to keep your mouth rinsed and less smelly.

If all else fails, rinse out your mouth in the bathroom or discreetly chew some gum.

very berry in love

*under 150 calories

Brimming with berries, this sexy Valentine's Day cocktail is even better than being hit by Cupid's arrow.

¼ cup mixed fresh (or thawed frozen) blueberries, raspberries, and strawberries

1½ ounces Skinnygirl Meyer Lemon Vodka or other lemon-flavored vodka

2 ounces Strawberry Lemonade Skinnygirl Sparklers or other diet fruit soda

Splash of sparkling water

Fresh blackberries, for garnish

Lemon wedge, for garnish

Muddle the blueberries, raspberries, and strawberries in the bottom of a rocks glass. Top off with vodka, soda, ice, and a splash of sparkling water. Garnish with a few blackberries and a lemon wedge.

the bitter breakup
*under 150 calories

Going through a rough breakup? It's time to call all your girls together for a cheer-up session. After all, when life gives you lemons, make lemonade—or, in this case, lemon cocktails!

1½ ounces vodka

3 ounces fresh lemonade

1½ ounces strawberry or strawberry juice blend

Tangerine or orange wedge, for garnish

Combine the vodka, lemonade, and juice over ice in a tall (highball) glass and stir until mixed. Garnish with a tangerine or orange wedge.

the orange crush
*under 150 calories

Whether it's a new baby or a wedding around the corner, showers are a great way to honor one of your girls. Serve this fresh and fruity drink, which works just as well without the booze if you've got any mommies-to-be in the crowd. Just use club soda instead of vodka to add a little sparkle.

1½ ounces vodka

3 ounces peach juice or nectar

1½ ounces orange juice

Fresh cherries, for garnish

Combine the vodka and juices over ice in a tall (highball) glass and stir until mixed. Drop in a couple of cherries to garnish.

PARTY PREDICAMENTS

What to do if nobody will leave the kitchen?
Why do people always want to crowd themselves into the least convenient, smallest space in the house? To keep this from happening, don't give people a reason to be in there. Block off the kitchen or turn off the lights, and don't serve any food or drinks in there. I will often physically lead people into another room. Always keep the bar and the food in the room where you want people to gather.

arnold palmer
*under 150 calories

This is your go-to cocktail for any al fresco party. It's always a hit with guys, too, and it works just as well without the vodka if some of your guests aren't drinkers. I love to serve it in a mason jar. (They're larger than a typical cocktail glass, so multiply the recipe as necessary to fill them.)

½ ounce vodka

2 ounces unsweetened iced tea*

Splash of lemonade

Juice of 2 lemon wedges

Lemon wheel, for garnish

Combine the vodka, tea, lemonade, and lemon juice with ice in a cocktail shaker and shake well. Strain into a rocks glass filled with fresh ice. If you'd like, garnish the rim with a lemon wheel and throw in the spent lemon wedges as well.

*You can use almost any kind of tea—black, chamomile, green, whatever.

naked cosmo

*under 150 calories

Home shopping parties are an excellent way to have a blast with your girls while also scoring a bunch of nice things. So why not spice things up by hosting a lingerie or, ahem, intimate accessories party. Serve this racy cocktail to get everyone in the mood . . . to shop!

1½ ounces vodka

½ ounce triple sec or other citrus liqueur

1½ ounces white cranberry juice

Juice of ½ lime

Lemon twist, for garnish

Combine the vodka, triple sec, and juices in a cocktail shaker filled with ice and shake well. Strain the drink into the glass. Garnish with a lemon twist on the rim.

KEEP TABS ON COCKTAILS

In the chaos and conversation of a fun party, people tend to lose track of their glasses. So they grab another one, and another one, and pretty soon you've got half-empty glasses all over your house. It's nice to give guests a way to keep track of which drink is theirs. There are mason jars with chalkboard labels that would be great for an outdoor party. Or you can buy little trinkets to put on the stems of wine or martini glasses. However you do it, offering a cute, theme-appropriate way for people to write their name on their glass means they don't have to hunt for that half-finished cocktail they set down, and you don't have dozens of extra glasses to wash at the end of the night.

black-eyed susan

*under 150 calories

Spending a day watching the races? The mint julep is standard fare at any Kentucky Derby party, but mix it up a little bit with my take on the signature drink of the Preakness Stakes.

1½ ounces white rum

1½ ounces club soda

Splash of triple sec or other citrus liqueur

Splash of pineapple juice

Splash of orange juice

Lemon wedge or strip of lemon peel, for garnish

Combine the rum, soda, triple sec, and juices with ice in a cocktail shaker and shake well. Strain into a rocks glass filled with fresh ice. Garnish with a lemon wedge or strip of lemon peel.

skinnygirl snacks

Guacamole is a fun and versatile snack that fits in well at all kinds of parties. My healthier version cuts a lot of the fat while still giving your guests something filling and flavorful to munch on. Serve with a selection of tortilla chips, whole-grain crackers, and raw vegetables. I love serving them with the tortilla chips that I created for my Skinnygirl line. They come in enticing flavors like Salsa Verde and Sweet Thai Chili and are made with wholesome ingredients like ancient grains, quinoa, and flax seeds.

mock-a-mole

SERVES 4

1 avocado, peeled, pitted, and mashed

1 cup cooked green peas

¼ cup chopped fresh tomato

2 tablespoons chopped fresh cilantro, plus more for garnish

1 tablespoon chopped red onion

1 tablespoon chopped fresh parsley

2 teaspoons fresh lime juice

1 teaspoon Worcestershire sauce

1 teaspoon garlic salt

½ teaspoon ground black pepper

¾ teaspoon Tabasco sauce

Combine all the ingredients in a large bowl and blend with an immersion blender until smooth. Garnish with cilantro.

blueberry lemon squeeze
*under 150 calories

There is no better way to celebrate America's birthday than by filling your backyard with friends. Fire up the grill, serve this delicious cocktail, and get ready for fireworks.

1½ ounces Skinnygirl Meyer Lemon Vodka or other lemon-flavored vodka

2¼ ounces blueberry lemonade

Fresh or frozen blueberries, for garnish

Combine the vodka and lemonade over ice in a tall (highball) glass and stir until mixed. Garnish by dropping in a few blueberries.

white cherry sparkling punch
*under 150 calories

Whether you're throwing an upscale engagement party for one of your girls or planning your very own wedding, serving this elegant punch as your signature cocktail will make it a night to remember.

SERVES 15 TO 20

One 750 ml bottle Skinnygirl White Cherry Vodka or other cherry-flavored vodka

One 750 ml bottle Skinnygirl Prosecco or other sparkling wine

1 gallon low-calorie cranberry juice

2 lemons, thinly sliced

1. Chill the vodka, prosecco, and juice in their bottles overnight.

2. Just before you're ready to serve, combine them in a punch bowl or two large pitchers. Add plenty of ice and the lemon slices.

VARIATION: This looks extra stunning if you use a block of ice instead of cubes. It's easy to make one by freezing water overnight in a clean empty quart-size milk container. Just cut off the carton after the ice is frozen, and you're done.

a bloody delicious bloody mary
*under 150 calories

Sometimes after a long week, all you want is to do a little day drinking and unwinding with your girls—and that's why brunch was invented! Indulge your BFFs with one of this midday classic.

2¼ ounces Skinnygirl Cucumber Vodka or unflavored vodka

4 to 6 ounces vegetable juice, such as low-sodium V8

Dash of Tabasco sauce

Dash of ground pepper

Celery stalk, for garnish

Martini olive, for garnish

Cucumber slice, for garnish

Combine the vodka, vegetable juice, Tabasco, and pepper with ice in a pint glass and stir until mixed. Garnish with a celery stalk, and the olive and cucumber slice on a pick.

mommy juice

*under 150 calories

The endless summer is over and the kids are finally back in school. You've earned some serious child-free relaxation, and what better way to enjoy it than to kick back with this sweet treat that's only for the grown-ups.

1½ ounces vodka

1½ ounces club soda

Splash of peach schnapps

Splash of orange juice

Orange wedge, for garnish

Combine the vodka, club soda, schnapps, and juice over ice in a rocks glass and stir until mixed. Garnish with an orange wedge on a pick.

long island iced tea

Get all dolled up for a night on the town, but instead of going out, make it a girls' night in. Crank up your hottest dance mix and serve the cocktail that screams "Let's get this party started!"

½ ounce vodka

½ ounce gin

½ ounce light rum

½ ounce white (clear) tequila (100% agave)

½ ounce triple sec or other orange or citrus liqueur

2 ounces lemon Sour Mix (page 17)

Splash of cola

Lemon wedge, for garnish

Combine the vodka, gin, rum, tequila, triple sec, and sour mix in a cocktail shaker with ice and shake until well chilled. Strain over fresh ice in a tall (highball) glass or mason jar. Top it off with the cola and stir once. Garnish with a lemon wedge on the rim.

┌ MAKE YOUR OWN PLAYLIST ─────

You can't have a good party without good music, especially if you want people to dance—and why wouldn't you?! You don't need to hire a DJ, just spend a little time on making your party playlist. When picking songs, consider the tone you want to set and the age of the guests—you'd probably play something very different for an all-ages hangout than you would for an adult dance party. It's nice to ease into things, starting with lighter music to encourage mingling and moving to more danceable tunes later in the party. Mix it up, too. You don't want it to be all disco or all classic rock. If you need some help, use services like Pandora and Spotify to create mood-specific playlists for almost any kind of occasion.

THE
HOLIDAYS

"

Holidays are a great reason to celebrate—but they can usually leave you feeling like you've gone a little overboard. Be smart and skip the famous holiday hangover by serving your guests hearty but healthy food and these guilt-free Skinnygirl delights. You'll have just as much fun, but everyone's spirits will be a little brighter in the morning.

white cranpire blood martini

You don't need to be a Scarygirl to love this creepy Halloween cocktail.

SERVES 2 TO 3

16 ounces Skinnygirl White Cranberry Cosmo

1½ ounces vodka

½ cup frozen blackberries

Black licorice twists, for garnish

Combine the Cosmo, vodka, and blackberries in a blender and blend until smooth. Strain into chilled martini glasses. Garnish with black licorice.

mulled wine

*under 150 calories

This cold-weather classic gives guests a very warm welcome and fits right in at any kind of winter party—from Thanksgiving to New Year's Eve.

SERVES 5

One 750 ml bottle Skinnygirl Cabernet Sauvignon or other red wine

3 cinnamon sticks, broken in half, plus 5 whole sticks for garnish

1 tablespoon whole cloves

3 star anise pods

1 whole nutmeg, cracked with the side of a chef's knife into a few pieces

Agave nectar, as needed

Peel of 1 orange, removed in strips with a vegetable peeler

1. Pour the wine into a large saucepan and place over low heat. Make a sachet with the cinnamon sticks, cloves, star anise, and nutmeg by tying them in cheesecloth. Add the sachet to the wine and simmer for 30 minutes, until the flavors are well combined.

2. Add agave nectar to taste. Strain the wine into heatproof glasses. Garnish each glass with a cinnamon stick and a strip of orange peel.

peppermint martini

No one can resist a minty glass of holiday cheer.

5 ounces Skinnygirl Bare Naked Vodka or other vodka

Splash of peppermint schnapps

Splash of club soda

Mini candy cane, finely crushed, plus 1 short peppermint stick for
  garnish

Combine the vodka and peppermint schnapps with ice in a cocktail shaker
and shake well. Rim a martini glass with water and the crushed candy. Strain
the drink into the glass and garnish with the peppermint stick.

naughty nog

*under 150 calories

This version of the Christmas standard is rich in creamy deliciousness without being rich in fat and calories.

SERVES 6

2 large egg yolks

⅓ cup sugar plus 1 tablespoon

2 cups 1% low-fat milk or soy or almond milk

1 teaspoon vanilla extract

Ground cinnamon

Dash of freshly grated nutmeg

2 ounces light rum

4 egg whites

6 cinnamon sticks, for garnish

1. Beat the egg yolks in a heatproof bowl until lightened in color. Add 1/3
cup of the sugar and beat until it dissolves; set aside.

2. Combine the milk, vanilla, and a dash each of the cinnamon and nutmeg
in a saucepan and place over high heat. Bring to a boil, stirring occasionally.

3. Remove the pan from the heat and gradually whisk the hot milk into the
egg yolks. Pour everything back into the saucepan. Return to the heat and
cook over high heat, stirring occasionally, until the milk mixture reaches
160°F on an instant-read thermometer.

4. Stir in the rum and pour into a clean bowl. Set the bowl in the fridge to
chill for at least an hour.

5. Just before serving, beat the egg whites in a clean bowl until soft peaks
form. With the mixer running, gradually add the remaining 1 tablespoon sugar
and beat until stiff peaks form. Fold the egg whites into the chilled mixture.
Sprinkle each serving with cinnamon and garnish with a cinnamon stick.

DRINKS INDEX

bethenny frankel is a four-time best-selling author. Her books include *Skinnygirl Solutions, Skinnydipping, A Place of Yes, The Skinnygirl Dish,* and *Naturally Thin.* She is the creator of the Skinnygirl brand, which extends to cocktails, health, and fitness, and focuses on practical solutions for women. She has been named one of the Top 100 Most Powerful Celebrities by *Forbes* magazine and is regularly featured in both *Health* magazine and *Glamour.* She is a graduate of the Natural Gourmet Institute for Health and Culinary Arts. Bethenny lives in New York with her daughter, Bryn, and dog, Cookie. Visit her at bethenny.com.

YOU CAN HAVE YOUR COCKTAIL AND DRINK IT, TOO.

Skinnygirl COCKTAILS is full of gorgeous, great-tasting, low-calorie cocktails (many under 150 calories) that add flavor and fun to any occasion. All the classics are here, from martinis to piña coladas, plus plenty of contemporary concoctions. Dip into this decadent collection of indulgent nightcaps, artisanal drinks, spicy and savory cocktails, and inspired infusions. Bethenny Frankel offers up all of the best of her signature drinks, including her:

- Spicy Jalapeño Margarita
- Ravishing Red Sangria
- Strawberry Basil Burst
- Naked Cosmo
- Peppermint Martini
- And many more

With everything you need to throw a fabulous party, including appetizer ideas, party planning tips, and the essentials for your home bar, *Skinnygirl Cocktails* is the last word in effortless entertaining.

COOKING/BEVERAGES   1014

COOKING BEVERAGES

ISBN 978-1-4767-7302-5   **$15.00 U.S./$18.00 Can.**

51500

9 781476 773025

TOUCH